R.C. Thomas loves language, his work is passionate and occasionally unsettling. He writes poetry with a sense of surrealist theatre, poems that are full of surprises. His writing offers unusual stories, visionary explorations and humour, told with steady confidence.

Rose Cook, author of *Taking Flight*

R.C. Thomas is an innovative poet and also a traditional one, not afraid of Latin prefaces but also capable of a rich colloquialism, a poet who employs a dense metaphoric language alongside a lyrical voice that takes the reader into new territory. In 'Flamingo' he strings together an almost Elizabethan richness of similes – 'tall social armpit sleeper' – that will delight the traditionalist; in 'The Colours of the Cat' he talks to his subject like an old friend: 'You clever old mousetrap of mystery'. He's innovative and experimental, bold and witty, a modern poet who carries his learning lightly and often spins it rhythmically around his head with the excitement of a genuine myth-maker:

I may find beauty and could sell my land,
move to the sea with five rings on each hand.

A poet to watch and enjoy.

John Daniel, author of *Missing the Boat, Grown Up War* and *Skinning the Bull*

He has long been one to watch, and with this strong, diverse collection Richard Thomas is now one to read. And reread. (2012)

I stand by what little I said, that The Strangest Thankyou was worth reading and rereading. These poems stay fresh for me, perhaps because they're not only about what they're about – whether flamingos or mermaids, pigeons or the

Immaculate Conception – they're about the discovery not just of their subject but of language and making, and the celebration of both. And they illustrate my favourite definition of poetry, that it is news that stays news. I like R.C. Thomas's attitude to his poems. He knows they're his but not his. The additions are excellent, so are the illustrations, and I extend a particularly warm welcome to 'The Do-Anythingness of Youth' that shows there's still depth in the old well and abundant scampi in the basket. The reissue of The Strangest Thankyou is good news. (2022)

Matt Harvey, author of *The Hole in the Sum of My Parts, Where Earwigs Dare* and *Careless Whisker*

R.C. Thomas's poems resonate with the essence of cool. The influence of the Beat poets echoes through this collection – yet each poem holds its own, revealing a unique illumination, vibrancy, playfulness and depth to the reader. Through fresh and sometimes surprising language, rhythm, structure, breath and flow, these poems summon their art to the mind's eye; the poet's deft and diverse use of form calling up duende, or channelling starlight, or creating by other means, impressionistic and abstract dimensions.

And amidst those forms there is a sensitive emotional intelligence; a mature man emerging through the wondrous and sometimes naïve perspective of youth, nurtured by, and amidst, and because of connections to the nature of Nature itself.

These lines from 'Nature' sum up this phenomenon, beautifully:

...and sunshine theories in my burning ears. Ah, gentle nature, how I long to be a part of you, take your oath and make a grand old oak.

Revisiting these poems in order to reflect on and update this endorsement after 10 years – I am struck anew with their loveliness and their wit. An absolute delight, brilliant.

Lucy Lepchani, author of *The Beckoning Wild* and *Lady-gardens*

R.C. Thomas's debut poetry collection embraces the magical and the mundane, the exotic and the everyday, the surreal rooted in reality.

Grand poetic themes of love, death and great lives are cut with surprising twists and playful use of language, shape, form and imagery. The poet seeks 'an array of wonder' in 'Dig' and spreads his 'riches' throughout The Strangest Thankyou.

Maria C. McCarthy, author of *As Long as it Takes*

R.C. Thomas is a real poet. His language is freshly squeezed from the poetry tube, rich in imagery, linguistically inventive, with veins of surrealism, romanticism (romanticism is not dead!) and compassion running through it. And yet it is conversational in tone, and there is humour in it.

This is a young man's poetry, exploratory, questioning, concerned with the truth even when apparently far off on a piece of fantasy. He knows where he is going. But he understands that what is important in poetry, and life, is not where you are going, but where you are. (2012)

Don't miss the haiku, written in Rome, which R.C. Thomas has added to this new edition. In my view, he has perfectly understood what the form and spirit of an English haiku should be. (2022)

James Turner, author of *A Chance of Love: Sonnets of Two Decades*

The poems of R.C. Thomas are dynamic and innovative... There's an intellect here which is happy to work with all kinds of emotions, and to explore the world he finds himself in through both the real and the surreal. His poems work on the page and in performance, not an easy thing to achieve. In R.C. Thomas's case, it's often through an innate lightness of touch.

Simon Williams, author of *The Magpie Almanack*

## THE STRANGEST THANKYOU (2012) REVIEW EXCERPTS

The poetry in the collection tells stories, and Richard Thomas does this in quite a few of his poems. These are not always linear stories but more so the experience of following the poet on a journey... The collection displays an emotional perception and a connection to nature, that only someone of Richard's poetic maturity could produce and be able to get away with.

Chris Gower, *Kettle and Yarn*

The writing of Richard Thomas is playful, self-aware and comical in one strand and artful, weighty and serious in another. These contrasting approaches wrap around one another throughout the book in a way that pulls the reader through the high reeds of his sometimes lyrical lake, twisting and tightening until you find your feet in his delivery. These poems are perfect for reading aloud and Thomas's eloquence bends the poems back and forth from how you experience them on the page, to how you hear him onstage.

Chris Muirhead, *London Grip*

Richard Thomas is a fresh young voice from Plymouth whose work combines a surprisingly direct yet engaging take on the surreal with a more romantic and passionate approach to his subject.

In 'Flamingo' for example, we are presented with a build-up of imagery which includes factual information, sharp observation, neatly given a skewed twist and a beautiful, terse lyricism which is both appealing and feels genuine, from the heart.

Thomas' work is a rare mix of the intellectual and the intuitive and it's a real pleasure to read, or hear read, as he's a fine performer of his poetry, also something of an unusual trait.

'...pinking the waters forever' has such a wonderful resonance and manages to avoid all the worst excesses of the over-laboured final line.

There's a clear sense of literary tradition in his work, whether that of the 20th century, as in the obvious surreal connections, or with an earlier romantic mode of writing. In 'Good Reason to Die', for example, there's a strong hint of an Elizabethan influence yet this is presented with such down-to-earth 'lack of flourish' which is both very funny and strangely moving.

This is a splendid debut collection and I'm sure we'll be hearing more from Richard Thomas in due course.

Steve Spence, *Stride*

R.C. Thomas (previously Richard Thomas) resides in Plymouth, UK, with his daughter. He has a BA in Creative Writing from Plymouth University. His first collection 'The Strangest Thankyou' (2012), and pamphlet 'Zygote Poems' (2015), were published by Cultured Llama, and his poetry and haiku have appeared in journals internationally. Of creative writing publications, he edited Symmetry Pebbles, was Managing Editor of INK, Plymouth University's creative writing journal, and he was the Creative Writing editor of Tribe, as well as Co-Editor of its sister publication, Thief.

**Web:** rcthomasthings.com
**Etsy:** etsy.com/uk/shop/RCThomasThings
**Instagram, Twitter, Facebook:** rcthomasthings

**SCAN ME FOR ALL LINKS**

## ALSO BY R.C. THOMAS

The Strangest Thankyou (2012, Richard Thomas)
Zygote Poems (2015, Richard Thomas)

# THE STRANGEST THANKYOU

R.C. THOMAS

10TH ANNIVERSARY EDITION

First edition published in 2012 by Cultured Llama Publishing

This edition first published in 2022 by R.C. Thomas Things



A CIP record for this book is available from The British Library

ISBN 978-1-3999-2847-2

Cover design and layout by R.C. Thomas

www.rcthomasthings.com

*For the do-anythingness of youth*

## CONTENTS

## FOREWORD: WELCOME TO A NEW EDITION OF THE STRANGEST THANKYOU

Richard Thomas is a poet who is not afraid to have some fun with language – as he is with illustration – but always, he makes the fun count. The poems in his $10^{th}$ anniversary edition of The Strangest Thankyou undoubtedly warrant this retelling, particularly as they are supported by a sparkling set of new poems and the poet's own bold and surreal illustrations, which throw fresh light on the text.

The pictures have some of the quality of jigsaws, but such puzzles were never like this before – they are mind mazes that flow in many directions. As for the poems, they also pay off some time spent dwelling within them, as opposed to just glancing over their surfaces. Twists and turns in the language make for innovation which seeds a refreshing dialogue between the poet and his audience.

In 'An Odd Response', Thomas deals skilfully with the problem of having been perceived an outsider while travelling in Italy, but all was resolved when

'Italian vocabulary dropped from the sky
and made a language on the ground'.

Still in Italy, six haiku, which are new to this edition, are beautifully counterpointed, line for line, in a way that creates that sought after haiku spaciousness:

no one to count the stars—
one side of Rome
to another

But tread carefully through the poem entitled 'Its'. It's an atlas of the surreal – a proper tour-de-force – squeezing into the tight corners of its own identity crisis, yet coming out footloose and content enough to begin again (very similar to the process of writing a poem, I should say!).

We stay with our feet anchored firmly in the surreal with the poem 'His Alarm', as it floats off in the dreamy yet nightmare world of our overdemanding consumer society with

... people asking people
(asking people asking people)
for stories and snacks

The final longer retrospective poem, 'The Do-Anythingness of Youth' has even more of a timeless visionary quality. Its sweep is appropriately wide and, as it looks back over the previous ten years of the poet's life, it is a dizzyingly linguistic achievement. I'd be a happy writer, if I could have a notebook like the one in section three of this lyrical soliloquy:

a notebook thick with fern,
a notebook bathed in patio...
a notebook gauzed in mist,
a notebook chalked with salt water...
a notebook soaked in daffodil,
a notebook masked in spring...
a notebook broiled in summer,
a notebook bright with beetle...

Susan Taylor, author of *La Loba Speaks for Wolf*

# INTRODUCTION

Dear Reader,

I wrote my first book of poems, as Richard Thomas, in my early twenties, wide-eyed, thick-haired, and wading through shrubbery like an eager thief in the night, hands stretched out before him for a grab-hold of the poet-candle. I swiped at every flicker of colour in the image of a poem that my peripheral vision could stretch to.

It has been ten years since releasing those poems into the wild and, so far, they have survived relatively intact (and it's a poem eat poem world out there). That's not to say they haven't needed feeding. A book of poems needs to keep up its strength. As such, I'm ensuring their nourishment with a slice of birthday cake, and offering them to you in a nice, new package.

To make it worth everyone's time, I've added some bonus features. Let me explain the differences between this 10th anniversary edition and the first edition published a decade ago.

*First difference: illustrations.*

Whether I am celebrating the beauty and dynamism of a flamingo, stream-of-conciousness-ing a horse eating mine-strone soup or prodding a tender finger at the rawness of the heart, they're all connected. As such, I have created nine montages to stitch the poems together.

*Second difference: poems added.*

In Rome, I wrote ten poems. Only nine poems made it into the first edition. The missing poem, 'An Odd Response', was considered lost for almost a decade. Between an original copy of the manuscript, courtesy of Cultured Llama, and discovering an old recording made by Bryce Dumont, who ran the bookshop-cafe come live-poetry-venue Epicentre in Paignton, UK, said poem is now back in action and 'An Odd Response' can now be found where it should be, here among its poem friends. You will also find some haiku from Rome, which I had set aside for a different book, but time shifts, life's change, and so here you can have them. Gobble them up.

'Its' and 'His Alarm' are two poems that were written at the time of compiling the first edition. Removed by my unrelenting inner critic at the last minute, they did not make the final cut. I have now come back to them, seen their beauty (I drop to my knees for forgiveness for dismissing them way back when), pulled them apart and put them back together again in a semblance both similar and unsimilar to their former selves, one that recalls my *then* and still placates my *now*.

As a way of a premature retrospective of the *Strangest Thankyou* era of life, I've included "The Do-Anythingness of Youth', written over the course of this A.D. 2022.

I hope this edition will be taken in the spirit of a young man in his early twenties, obsessed with each world each poem has to offer. That is to say, with a keen curiosity and delight in discovering each crevice language has to expose, and the openness to accept that the pig could be a mountain, as much as the mountain could be a swan.

Sincerely,

R.C. Thomas

## NATURE

Ah, sweet abstract of trees, I see through you to the mammoth star spilling itself over life beyond, seeping through your wiry fingers, washing your wild green hair in its enigmatic light - I'm not sure what it tells me.
And when the woodpecker with its beady eyes like buttons on a feathered case clicks and clacks against your hollow bodies - clicky click clack clack clucky click clack – I have a heart that says 'Take up that tempo.'
Every weekend I pass your life by and can't help but feel I should be more involved – to be a part of your rustic reverie, your naturalistic splendour would be wonderful - but I take this train quite regularly and forever
find myself perched on the side that pursues towering grey pylons, potent pike and potholes of a bumpy, battered track, and the morning mist clambers up to my windowpane on the carriage of grim diligence
and gives me nothing more than a loathsome glare, shakes its old cloudy head at me and whispers daisy thoughts and sunshine theories in my burning ears. Ah, gentle nature, how I long to be a part of you, take your oath and make a grand old oak.

## GOOD REASON TO DIE

In an all-white sun I sleep
figureless, moving closer to myself,
to which the Star Sisters hit me up with:
'Wake from that in which you lie!'
and so I wake and groggily reply:

'But the sun is going to die,
so I shall sleep on and go out with it,
a loyal ember, a promise I'll keep,
and then I can come back as snow
and be divine in my all-white flow.'

To which the Star Sisters reply
as quick as a comet: 'Fair enough.'
The sun fades like a mouldering orange,
I sweat my juice, I melt my mind,
and become the purest snow, divine,

and the Star Sisters whiten their shine
and the seas and soil are that of sheepskin -
in such aesthetic the world is shushed,
a candescent calm hushes through the universe
and all people everywhere make love to this verse.

## COLD PARK DAY

A cold sunshine day has occurred,
I see a spaniel chasing a blackbird,
grinding its squeaky gnashers
as the blackbird takes a perch on the sun.
A Winter-Summer day,
a Boxing Day-walk day
when all nature is being divine
and family leisure does thrive and shine.
And though the spaniel is not fireproof
he jumps onto the sun after the blackbird,
and feathers are made redundant,
and so a waft of burnt beak
smokes out the park and its people.

A man made of tree floats to me
with a dense melancholy for all to see.
I think surely he knew the blackbird,
it's surely obvious,
just look at his branches drooping,
the dew built up in his bark
and the gloom he's left on the park.
No, that is not the reason at all,
to the blackbird he acts indifferently,
it's to the weather he owes his melancholy,
and it seems he just wants to give me
a paraffin apple he's grown by tree.

The spaniel is alert with flame ears
and his owner looks at him with tears,
for he has forgotten to fetch a stick
and instead has a worm in his mouth.

I feel a worrying chill coming on,
so I eat my apple
and stove myself,
becoming a rustic kind of warm.

The spaniel on fire comes to me and together we keep doubly warm,
the owner wipes away his tears and puts his hands out to relish our heat,
and so all three of us lament the blackbird, breathing the waft of burnt beak,
whilst the man made of tree floats back and takes up a new melancholy.

**STILL,
PEACEFUL
NIGHT AND
SOMEWHERE
OUT THERE
A BOULDER
HAS THE
WOODSMAN'S
TOE TRAPPED:**

gorging
moonflow
over the
forest like
snow light/
egg white
on skyward/
nightward
rusting
pins and
a woodsman
chops off
his big
toe and
gratefully
breathes
in his
release to
a new
toeless
world
and
the sharp
cry
of his
mother's
voice:

'Freidel!
Freidel!
My
foot, it
is a
stump
too.'

## THE CHASE

Hot soil of day; dry dirt
of day; glorious gleam
over mountains; death

of day is night; still air
of night; dark blue hum
that thickens; death

of night is day; twenty
four hour chase;
seasonal loop; death

of day is day; constant
rotating battle; fight
for Earth's attention; death

of night is night; all ends;
Sun droops its eyelids;
champion the Eclipse.

## TOY FOR A LOVELESS CHILD

What is lemon folly

but games of a yellow dolly?

Blonde-haired toy of fruit tree

suns her game in Sicily,

bored.

the woodpecker with its loyal snow toe gorging on night all day

# THE COLOURS OF THE CAT

Little black cat waiting for me to step
outside my door before I've gone to make
a step out - this time I've done a window check,
seen you there like darkness – a feline wake.
In blips of cool summer rain you are there
to purr, to fur my legs within your weave,
in magnificent beams of sunlight dare
to yolk your yellow diamond eyes then leave.
But wait, black cat you've become a white cat
having high heaven's angelic eyes out
with tail-whip of an albino cat -
a magic creature? I very much doubt.

You clever old mousetrap of mystery,
colour is inapt, you still unnerve me.

## GARDEN CAT

I've spotted you lurking again,
little black cat,
but this time in my Mother's back garden
doing vertical hops
over the heather,
running quick circles in your sheer excitement.
The mentality of you
scampering
all this way from home is astounding.

You must have followed me
up on the train, cat -
to spy on me or seek out the geraniums?
Either way,
I feel on edge.
But how you take the whole garden in,
the freshness of it,
breathing in
what you so desirably own.

You know, Mother's neighbours
also need a cat.
As I hook my head up and over the fence,
I see their empty
angel of a lawn
and their dead princess of a patio.
Which crying child
that wakes me
at dawn do you so deny?

I imagine a child to yearn
for a little black cat
like a child should yearn for their mother.
You should go
and fulfil their needs.
I'll miss your jumps and larks on the lawn,

but a cat won't dress me
and make my bed,
nor keep me content forever.

Come back with wild purr
and virtuoso
ringing collar
when suited for another poem.

# FLAMINGO

Flesh-coloured shrimp-eater,
wide-winged wired bird,
raking the dirt pedalling the earth,
knee-knobbled beanpole legs,
knee being ankle joint,
long wavy bright length,
herds of necks pushed right back,
heads out, all in one leg,
vibrancy-curved pink spinner,
beak in the ground like a compass,
dot-eyed wading follower,
feather-liced idoliser,
tall social armpit-sleeper,
delightful eyeful not quite parrot,
ancient Roman delicacy,
great poignant egg defender,
living embodiment of Ra,
popular plastic lawn ornament,
iconic worshipped filter-feeder,
underwater insect-sucker,
upside down water-drainer,
thirty seven miles per hour flapper,
Africa North America
Central America Europe
South America Asia,
lava-loving ice bird,
mud-mounder by mouthful,
cunningly undesirable,
thirty years of male looking female,
thirty years of female looking male,
many accidental bisexual nights,
lethargy-enthused strawberry sunset
pinking the waters forever.

## KINGDOM

*After Nature's Myth by Catherine Bleck*

The cheetah is eyeing up the elephant,
the elephant is sorrowing the whale,
the whale is eager to get away from it all
and is quick to dart under the turtle,
the turtle thinks he can fly
and never hit the elephant's head,
but the parrot, he's so cocksure,
he makes a seat of the elephant's head!
and the parrot is waving to the killer whales,
the killer whales are fleeing from the rhino,
the rhino is being stalked by the gazelle,
who has got that innocent childlike look
as if to say 'Me? I'm not doing anything,'
and I'm thinking: you better do something
because the tiger has got his eye on you,
and the whale is going to whip your horns off
with a combination of wave and tail,
and he's slinging a shark down on top of it all,
the poor shark's never looked so helpless!
The tiger, he's on top of it all,
the tiger thinks he's got it sussed,
but there's a bird in the top left corner of the world
quietly making a master plan.

## BIRTH AND/OR DEATH OF A SEASON

I found a new Spring in my loft
laid out amongst the dust of old Spring.
There she was, sobbing,
so I asked her: 'Spring, why so sad?'
and Spring said: 'It's old Winter,
he's dying, he's become weak.'
'Oh Spring,' I said, 'it's only natural,
don't be sad, young season,
he's dying for you to blossom,

it's your turn now, Winter's nodding,
but don't worry,' I said, 'it's only natural,
and we'll always remember
those snow-white blanket days
with children finding fun
in slurping icicles,
who'd have thought their tongues should stick -
how logical;
and the forest as ghostly as it had ever been,
how it looked like a gloomy haunt
from some zombied Hansel-
and-Gretel-esque picture book,
and the squirrel peeking out a frosty nose
but returning with a tremor
for the acorn at his bedside -
what fond memories we shall have of Winter;

but now, Spring, it's you,
come, see the cheer,
now it's up to you to carry Winter's urn.
How proud the other seasons shall be
to see you bless a dead Winter
with the green you shall live.
Go, Spring, hurl yourself
upon the small requests
of the licking lambs,

let them sneak, draw close and suck,
let them nourish you, Spring,
and Spring, nourish them in return,

and go breeze the old, ratty,
cantankerous attics everywhere,
waft the cobwebs with your sweet sleek breath,
blow them to the heavens like spider kites,
and Spring, grace us your primrose kiss,
seduce us your modest tulip
and create, Spring, create
soft yellows, greens and blues,
that will make us the true earthen figures
of your pastoral beauty.
Let us have the bemused mole,
his eyes full-wide awake,
let us see the once shy shrew
rediscover his confidence,
and the hare, oh boy, the hare,
he'll be beside himself,
won't know what to do,

the beaming of the sun
may shed some light,
some modesty, some mind
and maybe he'll get his act together
and beat the tortoise after all,
leap the finishing line
with a loud 'Spring, I race for thee!'
Ah, Spring, my tender Spring,
all the optimism you may bring...'

So then Spring, no longer weepy,
but with her eyes now full-bright,
got on with being Spring
with a wealth of Easter about her
and no more sorrow for Winter,
but only fond memories,

and I dared not mention
her inevitable burden
of a Summer's day.

## THE WILD ORDER OF THINGS

A little naked Inuit girl
in the hallow light of a full moon,
a wolf tucked under arms,
its soft fur stroking her tanned and goose-bumped skin,
her father cooks a salmon over the fire,
its skin splits, spilling pink upon the stretched flames,
he wonders what shade the wolf will spill.

The wolf's tongue takes to her arms,
its tail wrapped around her slender hips,
she pulls the wolf tight,
her father stops at the fish,
but knowing tomorrow's menu
a drop runs down the hills of her cheeks,
splashes and glistens the wolf's pebble nose.

sorrowing strawberry over the

fire

with

licking

lambs check the

cat

lurking

in

the

## THE VALLEY HELD NO RELIGION

From the tip of a mountain the woman dove,
 giving herself generously to God's hands,
  and swinging to and fro she fell
  like a feather in a breeze.

A dozen spectators spectacled her stunt
 from the bottom of the long snowy mountain,
  and when beautifully landed,
  yelled 'Inspect her spine and ribs.'

And sure enough they found her soft and bird-like,
 and so God retired his hands embarrassed -
  they weren't needed by the woman
  who defied the mountain's height.

## EVERYDAY A CRIMINAL

I shot a car into the air and cried,
for that following night all vehicles died,

so I laid lilies and ointments down on the highway
and the tarmac obliged and I had my way,

I said I'd be good but I made a bomb
and the next thing I knew the whole world was a bomb,

it seemed terrorism had become quite ordinary,
which was a shame, but I got on with my daily activity.

## STEALING

I stole two hundred pounds,
I'm not sure what to do with it -
I could buy some new shoes with it,
or a fat gold-plated watch
and count down the hours
before I'm found out.

## CÉZANNE AND HIS CRITICS

Down long Parisian streets,
steeped with sepia
and seeping Seine,
he went,
canvas stacked on back,
hobbling hunchback,
like He of Notre Dame
or Christ with his crucifix.

'I am the Messiah,' he yelled
and no one believed him,
even gargoyles laughed
from their cloisters
at his paintings
of pottery and naked bathers.
Gaining closer to the gallery,
the critics saw his coming,

scorned and pitied -
poor Paul Cézanne
was to walk back home,
the saddest walk of them all,
acrylic weeping in tow,
too much brushstroke for them,
too un-classical.
Ah, but little did they know

that one hundred years on
his hatted card players
with white pipe would have gone
for one hundred and sixty million,
and I can hear Cézanne
rolling in his grave with laughter,
yelling
'That'll show the bastards.'

## SOUP CHRONICLE #1

There must be some action
with the secateurs
to slice and chop together
a garment that I can don
whilst the butcher mushes meat
down on the dancefloor,
and a white horse waits
for me at the table.
And when the fine lady
in her swan white dress
finally gets herself together
and asks me to dance,
there must be some action
in our china faces
that grow paler as the butcher
starts on the sausages.
And as our feet trace
the final waltz,
there must be some action
with the white horse
who'd been left at the table
slurping on soup
and gets wind of horse meat
and realises he's a delicacy -
on ending the dance
the butcher pulls out a knife
with a big H on it
and the horse is now behind us
breathing minestrone breath
down our bare necks.
And there must be some action
in our final waltz,
so the fine lady and I
kiss softly and sweetly,
and the deep squelch
of what goes on behind us

and the off smell of horse death
becomes a little more bearable.
And now there must be some action
in the fresh soil
to wrap a horse body tight
and hold it in place.

## BEAUTY REALLY

They fear the hit of baseball cap girls
and gather noisily under sticky bridges,
passively cursing the night's activities,
shaking their loose sweating skins
with a peculiar distance in their eyes,
but no one quite knows why;
but to slip a slinky petticoat on,
oh don't they look wonderful,
such a tall, dark city they give themselves to
and such lonesome lovers they become;
and to think, they eat figs at night,
                                        how romantic,
and how kind of Bella to pet the frothing dog
that comes to them salivating and helpless,
                                        and Anna feeds it a fig.

## THE FLOWER POT

*Scenes cut out from an unknown film and rewritten*

The servant stumbles out of the door
with a crate of bottles and clunks it down
in a mushroom cloud of dust.
Here comes the man of the house,
he pushes the servant against the wall,
he asks him where the girls went
and threatens to choke the servant
when he says he doesn't know anything.

* * *

The girls are in the ocean-blue Chevy,
with lips tightly locked
upon one another's lips,
trembling, kissing,
and all the while pretending to drive.

* * *

The two girls are alone in a sandy bedroom.
A dusty, flowered quilt seats them
for the rounder to be denied by the angular
who wears the ocean-blue dress,
who has her hand slipping, sliding away
like a snake out from her marriage.
They kiss anyway (fancy that!)
and are disturbed by the wail of a baby.
Oh, passion! They kiss once more,
full saliva, sunblushed lips
part and close, part and close.

* * *

Through the shadows comes the man of the house
clouded over in a strong monochrome.
He comes home and asks his wife
if she's had her driving lesson today.
'No.' He fits with anger and wakes his son
with his hands pounding down hard upon
the kitchen table, and then the violation
of his wife's long, limby body.

* * *

A smashed flower pot, soil spilt out
over the cracked clay and onto the pavement,
like an overdue volcano having finally erupted.
The girls have got their hats on, smiling.

the
hours
from
a
meat
mountain
there
must
be
gargoyles
in
two
lilies
following
H

## BAD MOVIE

I've been watching someone else's movie
like a moving picture voyeur
smug for my guilt-free nosiness.

From my seat across the aisle
I've seen the gunslinger in his excitement
put a bullet to the jackal.

I've smelt the gunpowder spread
in the stale air as I heard the jackal
howl long, high and smooth.

The man whose screen it is
and to whom the movie belongs
seems unmoved in comparison to me.

I wonder if he pays attention at all?
I feel I should walk across to his seat
and tell him: 'You should be moved.

A jackal has been shot, poor dog.'
But then I'm stopped in my path;
another jackal has been shot.

Blood shoots from its twitching abdomen
like a hose of red wine – I won't bother,
no, it's just an unimaginative movie.

Besides, the gunslinger has grown weary
and all that's left to do now
is blow his own brains out.

A slow stream of thick red syrup
creeps across an icy stone floor,
trickling to meet a dead jackal's leg.

## PUTTING THE POEM IN DANGER

Last night,
on the patio,
a student was talking
about those who have killed,
he then went on to say
he would play murder
like a drinking game:
after every killing,
he, the killer,
would swallow another shot.
To me this seemed like
a poor excuse
to become an alcoholic,
and in fact,
a poor excuse
to kill;
if you ask me
this seemed like
a poor excuse
for a one way conversation,
and I am beginning
to realise that
*this* might seem like
a poor excuse
for a poem;
this poem
will probably be
the first in line
if I'm not careful,
so I'm putting the pen down
and hiding this one
amongst the rest -
safety in numbers.

## 160 CHARACTERS A POEM

### WHY, WHY

with both my eyes
do I see my
hen telling lies
to my kind, shy,
toothless fox?
And why, why
with weary eyes
do I try
to take in why
my hen's changed the locks?

### A DEAD CLOCK ON THE WALL,

a bone white lily wilting,
an empty mint-tinted wine bottle,
and from beneath the bin
crawls the money spider
spinning a new vitality web.

### INFINITY BINDS INFINITY,

eyes rope in eyes,
new adventurers
kill old adventures.
A wide forest:
16 lovers meet
and see in the milkiness
of a new moon
with mass suicide.

## A CLOCK'S FUNCTION

The second is the switch,
the minute the second's bitch,
the hour counts the face
its sixtieth disgrace,
the clock all in all
makes old the young fool.

## THE TEARMAKER

My squishy eyes produce the mildew
upon the reddening crust of a bitten lip,
on a poor wage.

I could have made better than tears:
dreamy blaze of sun throat,
preferably.

## THE TEAR

The drop that drips down the plump, twitching cheek
magnifies the skin with a salty ooze.
Water that gathers in the cracked face creek -
the joy of Earth we're afraid to lose.
The make-up destroyer filled with hot rage,
an anti-mascara duct causing pain,
putting black gunk on the writing punk's page -
but how dare it play such a tactless game?
The poor eye is bathed and the face is splashed -
agony, the sea of the human face,
waves of anger and brutal times have clashed
as the eyelid swims from the sad salt's chase.

The eye shall close soon in great heaviness,
open at daybreak in half of the mess.

a
bitten
lip
the
drinking
jackal
killing
my
hen
with
the
fox
upon

## HORSE OF TREVI FOUNTAIN

At the back of Palazzo Poli I stand,
sun veering down upon the taming of water,

I go

to throw ten cents into the Trevi Fountain,
'Can I hit the horse on the head?' I ask,

I throw

and the horse pushes out his long horsey neck,
and with the whip of a tongue gulps the coin right down.

I know

that he had been hungry for a good many years,
but now as I look the horse straight in his marble-eyes,

I know

he's a bellyful better off for swallowing my coin,
and with a smile on my face for my throwing to his charity,

I go...

## AN ODD RESPONSE

I asked a signor his name, but he just let out
some inconceivable cackle.
I was dumb to the cackle.
I stood there on the piazza feeling
the dust thicken on my tongue.
I spat out a lousy dust cloud.
I fiddled my hands in my hair
and pulled, and handing him a strand said:
'English hair.'
He was dumb to the hair.

He stood there on the piazza asking
the Mafia what had just happened before him.
Getting the nod from Michael,
he put his hands up to the sky
and pulled apart the night like a purse.
Italian vocabulary dropped from the sky
and made a language on the ground.

I scooped up the language
and put it in my pocket.
No longer dumb, I repeated the question:
'Come ti chiami?'
It came from my mouth Italian, no problem.
The signor went to cackle,
but he was dumb to his own cackle
and choked on a muted voice.
I had won the contest, and to compensate,
I reached into my good nature
and gave him the words 'Beauty' and 'Kindness'
to dwell on.

## WHAT KEATS AND SHELLEY SHOWED ME

*On visiting the Keats-Shelley House, Rome*

Wilde's handwriting, tall, wiry and slim
danced across the browning page.

Shelley's broken jawbone sat in an alabaster hold
amongst the books of yesteryear -
what old, sacred air that jaw must have chewed upon.

Keats' death mask, blank and balding in the bedroom,
gaunt, ghostly expression of dying -
life had been sucked from him, I saw it then
in those hollowed eyes before me.

Whitman had put his thoughts down,
wild scrawl of relentless motion.

Lord Byron was everywhere!
with carnival mask pretending to be a brute,
he popped up in the container,
and on the anonymous page he even appeared.

And whose hair was that dried in a lock,
holding politics but John Milton's.
and Elizabeth Barratt, her hair there too -
sweet to hairdress the deceased.

# ARISE TO THY LYRE

*On visiting The Protestant Cemetery, Rome*

Spirits steam
from the soil
like Heaven's own perfume;
only the poets can make death
smell sweet.

I want
to throw my eyes
upon the graves of them
and seize an illumination
of words.

I sit
beneath an air
rich with archaic shades
thinking of the romantics who
ate beef.

## HAIKU

no one to count the stars—
one side of Rome
to another

walking for days—
the dead poets
here all along

Roman arch—
an old beggar sits
frowning at girls

riding home—
the last Colosseo
station gladiators

sun strokes—
tourists brushing
by the fountain

lightening with each step
morning climbs
up to the church

## WHAT BETTER THING TO SEE?

What better thing to see
when sipping cappuccino in Barberini
than not just one black nun but three,

divine as angels in their white gowns,
there's not the slightest frown
on any sweating face around,

for there's nothing to frown for when you see
three nuns happily
adorning gold sunglasses in Barberini.

Oh, joy that they bring to the mindful eye
as they gracefully pass us by
with grinning complex that alights the sky,

and I can feel their smiles upon me,
the gleam of their brows upon me,
the drips that drown me under the sun so holy.

The last sip of caffeine has now become richer,
entranced we are by this holy picture,
and think 'What better thing to occur?',

and what better thing to see
when sipping cappuccino in Barberini
than sweet and poignant, natural beauty.

## TWO PIGEONS

*In Rome, watching two pigeons: 'You know what that is? Greed...gluttony.' - David Mullens*

Two pigeons.

No wind, only dust.

Dry air.

Six crumpled cigarette butts.

One slice of pizza coated in dust.

Two pigeons.

Mangled claw pigeon

And healthy claw pigeon.

One slice of pizza coated in dust.

Bam!

Healthy claw pigeon goes for it.

Pecks at it like a madness.

Two pigeons.

One slice of pizza coated in dust.

Mangled claw pigeon wants to share.

Mangled claw pigeon loses an eye for asking.

Gluttony!

Sin in the city of holiness.

**NO DREAM**

They come at me emerging
from the slow heave of tourists, they come,
two bronze figures, hair like strands of horse tail,
black, coarse upon the sky's ghostly hue, they come.

Their feet barely grace the ground
as they skip towards me, hands held, swinging,
they come at me like surrealism,
and just as peculiar, like two spirits, they come.

A playground portrayal of mother and daughter;
I pause, holding up the morning's traffic
to immerse myself in the song they sing:
'Si morta Madelena, che si morta fa?' they sing.

'Madeline is dead, why did Madeline die?'
and so the song they sing rolls on heaven-bound,
like a scene from an old arthouse movie
it rolls on and they pass me as they sing.

## MARY

*On seeing the* Immaculate Conception *in the Trinità dei Monti, Rome*

She's unstirred in her heaven,
staying calm in the clouds,
holy like a dove, a dove, a dove.

The blue that's draped upon her
like a vast ocean that rolls smoothly
bathes your eyes of the Hell you've seen.

She's not mistaken for another woman,
though her soft features may be deceiving,
she remains unspoilt: a truth, an honesty.

There's the Catholic who proudly weeps
as they put another candle before her,
and the cynics that envy their belief in perfection.

And there are the young angels' glad faces,
which seemingly appear from nowhere
like little lights in the background behind her.

What persistence she has,
appearing not only in the Trinità dei Monti
but many other churches all over.

The sun that blazes is questionable,
as no matter how close she stands before it
her back never browns nor goldens.

This is for she is the pale beholder of life,
giving and given inseparable
in its purest and untainted form.

## CANNULA CHILD

The air pushes down on the piazza like a furnace,
there's hush for our sweating, we monsters in our bodily
muck.
But child that yells, oh child that yells!
no hush for the child that is tied to his chair by a tube,

like a crazy vine. Strangled by tube, poor child,
his face colouring like a plum as he yells,
oh how he yells, hear that child yell!
Dave Mullens and I, sat in the shade, scratch out our note-
books in fury,

knowing how useless we are to his gloom,
a colossus of tube and child and veins.
Child that yells and yanks back and forth!
A madman lashing out for sanity in his jungle,

restrained from pleasure and play.
An ugly day, the peacemaker has lost his place here.
Nose glowing child, child that swells!
The air snatches multitudes of breath from trembling lips,

his lips waver like an orchid's petals in the rainless storm.
No mercy on the piazza today, just swathes of heat
and a child's yell, such a raw yell!
His sickness seems to thrive in the heat of Roman day

and leaves him savage-tempered and restless,
poor child that yells, many miserable yells!
If only there was something to bring him comfort and
calm -
his mother gives him a weary toy.

## OUTSIDE OF THE FOUR-STAR RESTAURANT

Outside of
the four-star
restaurant,
a lonely
pigeon shudders
at the signorina's
bronze feet,
pigeon-

ill, falls on-
to his back
and still in
spasm, flicks
himself upright and moves
along.
So hard is
the day

that descends
upon his
dry, dirty
feathers that
flutter at her
feet for romance that the
poor, lost
pigeon

loses his
birdish self-
composure.
Pigeon, I
too demand some
affection, I too am
pigeon-
ill. The

sun heats him
on the curb,
he thrusts his
neck out for
love. I, pigeon,
thrust my soul for the same
thing, and
whilst

humans cast
their power
on his back
just like a
distant stranger
casts an icy stare, a
weighty
stone on

the mind, I
feel the
pigeon twitch-
ing in my
crooked ribcage.
If I, pigeon, were a
bird, I
could love

you, or if
you, pigeon,
weren't a bird,
you could love
me. But, alas,
holiday or grand arch-
itec-
tural

nest, sweetness
of mine or
meek outlook
of yours, we
go on, pigeon-
ill, two thrust-out beings
in an
aching

eternal
all-craving
existence,
searching for
the same wholly
celestial state to
fill our
souls and

with the same
desire
to peck our
way through life
for a fulfilled
companionship, yet two
very different beings
indeed.

my eyes the unstirred pizza in a carnival mask sweating a language beneath

# DIG

Should I dig some more of the earth today?
What shattered lighthouse bulb and what riches
should my shovel clank amongst the decay?
The brittle bones laid about in ditches
make each treasure I find more exciting
comparing it with the cracked skull I shook
in my cupped hands after Monday's digging,
or Tuesday's find of a fisherman's hook.
There's got to be an array of wonder
scattered below amongst the stinking dead,
if I just root underneath a shoulder
of a farmer's loved one who'd never wed.

I may find beauty and could sell my land,
move to the sea with five rings on each hand.

## ROAD

Your road, sad road, smoke road:
road that shoots through carcass-rot,
and either side red soil heaved up,
crumbling, sun-dried by everything.
Your road that narrows like a slug-end:
no favourite width road. Dandelion,

deflowering, sleepy in fumes. Dandelion,
suicidal on the side of city road
which paves its noisy way to end
in the calm of the ocean in great road-rot.
Road through farming-goodness in everything
like sweet root vegetables heaved up

by muddy men who prefer heaved up
natural taste to road-dead dandelion.
Your road feels it is all and everything;
no wild bear in a rainbow can stop road
in fear of becoming poor wildlife-rot
left in the rubble for the flies. An end

to your road is only the ocean. An end
isn't seeing cypresses heaved up
and left in a pile of decrepit wood to rot
like the poor merciful dandelion -
that's no feat as your wicked road
is capable of destroying everything.

Road that swerves: a serpent around everything,
and doesn't conceive to a passive end,
nor gives in to footpath beauty. Road:
unforgiving black-streaked tarmac up
and over rocky bridges kills the dandelion,
carrying the exhaust that makes dandelion-rot.

Dipping road that makes squished-rot
of the minute bugs that give their everything
in an attempt to cross in triumph – dandelion
falls withered warning them of their end.
Your road that grabs all and rips all up,
mapping the route of a deadly road.

Road, you are by no means everything,
you too will come to an end and rot
like the dandelion as the ocean chews you up.

## THE ARCTIC

Our boat sits politely in the stillness
of an Arctic afternoon. The netting
in a tattered mound, is lined with a new frost,

crystallised by our crisp and skeletal
backdrop. We bludgeoning men feel bare, stripped
of the hefty coats that had us pinned down

in maritime killing: weak silver flusters
struggling for a breath, our bullish way
of pounding them. But today's easy,

with empty minds and a glacial scope, mountains
whose peaks are lost in a cooling mist
blanketing the sky with alabaster -

Arctic, icy and angelic, flowing,
white; a baby drawing thin, tender
breaths in her fresh, uncreased christening gown.

## MERMAID

The mermaid's got my heart, she
swings it in a knot like
a bloody pendulum in the centre
of a heavy ocean,

I grow paler with her touch, her
slippery scales brush my pulse, I
feel salt-stings but what's forgotten
is the rotting of my sins.

On the ocean bed: used cotton,
rusting cans and strangeness, we
met for her to suck up my tears
and swim in the sorrow

that has me and all my fears
grounded, strangled by seaweed,
missing my innocent shore, my
maid who plops scallops in a basket.

## A LAND OWNER'S LAMENT

What, tsunami, have you done to have made
    palm trees lean
    like beckoning fingers bent
to a wasteland, to have smashed open coconuts,
    slinging them
    to the dirt as if they were dust?
My hands are still clutched onto this trunk,
    splinters deep
    beneath the cracked tips
    of my ageing fingers,
my toenails torn and bloodied by the wreckage
    you threw at me
    in your great concave,
and your thrashing water has bruised my chest.
    Tonight, tsunami,
two days on from your cold surge of sea,
    I am still here,
    clinging on to all I have left,
    my island is a mess.
Tsunami, all my vegetation, my mangos,
    my jackfruit:
all washed away in your deathly splash,
    and my cattle now sleep
    on soggy soil
without a single cattle-breath between them.

## SEA THIEF

My sea has now been stolen
by a thousand dulling rock pools
that dim her once bright waters.
What well could have been
with my sea has now been tainted
by bastard crabs that attack my sea,

pincers pulling and tugging.
I once sailed across her, proud,
like a brave, buoyant seagull:
my ship now hollowed out,
sorry in the thick and murk,
had once streamed right across

the bounce of her salty chops
with grace and gentle apathy.
My sea that has since been stolen
now laughs at me in the hold
of drying, haggard land.
Sea, well she could cheat on me

with the sky: remove the clouds,
and soak the sun - I'd realise
her need for elevation,
to crash into the cool arms of air.
But for my sea to splash the land
couldn't be forgiven.

## SONG FOR A SEASHELL

Perhaps, Seashell,
I was not made
to be loved.

Perhaps,
I have only you
to hold up to my ear,
head tilted,
gutted, listening

to the sounds of the ocean:
eel screams and lobster
bangs, the sounds
I have been deprived of.

Seashell, tell me
who sang my lament
before I came into being?

And, Seashell, who tolled
the bell of solitude
before I arrived,
dreaming
like a jealous child?

Perhaps, Seashell,
it's my good heart
that denies me
the ocean's kiss,

or, perhaps, Seashell,
being forlorn
with dry hands
secretly makes me happy.

in palm trees a road-dead

dandelion skull with a mermaid by the seashell lighthouse bloodied only

## HANDS

The space between my right hand
and my left hand
is vast.
Now, should I be so masculine
as to place a body
neat and tight
between my right hand
and my left hand
and hold it there
like an elder would hold a cracked vase,
would I not feel unsettled?
Would it not seem unnatural
to my deadened pulse?
Would my hands not jut so,
so much
that like the vase
that would spit one hundred dead flowers,
my hands would blow
the body up?
My love is an atom bomb;
my love is an atom bomb, surely.
Yet I seek to fill the space
between my hands,
yet I seek to put colour
back into my body once more,
to grow a red rose from my chest,
to become that romantic cliché,
yet I seek for my hands
to feel
and for some warm spirit to nurse me
with a damp cloth,
and yet I still seek for a body
to become present
between my right hand
and my left hand
regardless of whether

my love is atomic;
my love is atomic, surely.

# ITS

It bought It white lilacs,
It shoved petals in It's ears,
It snorted pollens,
It ate stems,
It was no longer human.
It held open doors,
It spooked into rooms,
It locked eyes with strangers,
It longed to be outdoors
where cold winds could wind It.
It bought It fancy dinners,
It painted cutleries black,
It cut wines,
It filled It's glasses with Achilles heels,
It craved vinegars.
It told It's self things,
It l a u g h e d,
It l a u g h e d,

It l a u g h e d,

It didn't know It's own jokes.

It held It's own hands,

It snapped It's own fingers,

It snared It's Achilles heels,

It made a series of crunches,

It'd not seen It's self smile before.

It tried to be more to It's liking,

It squashed It's face,

It groomed It's eyebrows,

It tidied It's veranda,

It's roof became It's floor.

It produced It mistletoe,

It replaced berries with garlic,

It sold It's mistletoe to a snared It

who gave It the crux of Archilles heels,

It spent the earnings on white lilacs.

## CUPID'S TOOLS

Great arrow of Companionship, you shoot us soulless -

no man good enough for you, heart blower.

Doused in Devillian blood you make your shot from
Cupid's high hopes -

we stand to snap you, may man render you bow-less.

And without aim or feathered finery streaming from
your flight

you'll be nought but another stick, splintered -

and it will be you, great arrow of Companionship, that
remains forever hopeless.

# LIFE AS A POEM

Sometimes writing poetry is hard,
I go to grab it but it's gone,
gone from my mind, slung its pompous self out the window.

Sometimes obtaining the contents of my own mind is hard
too,
I go to grab myself but I've gone -
I think perhaps I've gone out the window with the poetry.

My poems and my mind often rebel,
once I caught them making out in the bathroom,
another time they kept me up all night with their constant
squabbling;
and as sure as sometimes my words deny the page,
my heart denies my mind also and so forth.

This is not to say that there is never an easy poem, realise
that.

Yes, many a day have I awoken to look out of my window
and see the golden autumn leaves as Nature's seasonal
currency,
many old and gnawed bristles of a toothbrush have I seen as
a clutter of fish bones;
many a moment have I snapped up from my desk in some
great burst
to think: cotton hands! ocean stew! mad nuzzling eagle
stealth!

Yes, those images come in occasional flashes to embrace
the page,
no, more so: love the page, screw the page in its pale, linear
ass.
Well, if only my mind was as easy as those moment then,
just think, I'd understand myself more than you'd
understand me,

or you'd understand me more than I'd understand myself,
I don't know, either way it's similar.

So, I guess the conclusion I am trying to draw
is that what my life is now
is forever searching for those sweet images and mad word
combinations,
constantly looking for my life to become that eternally easy
poem.

## POOR HORSE POEM

The mourning horseman churns a weary weep.
Plodding hooves pivot upon the smoky floor like a drunk,
 drunk.
The Bleak Bosom heaves at the horseman's mind
as the dense mash of auburn leaves flutter in the sky.

He has arthritis of the candle-hip.
A bony mound of blackened wax melts slow, slow.
His cart carries the burden of the Bleak Bosom
with he, in his mourning suit: worn, pale, glum.

What long, Plasticine tongue should lick the day's bad hay
but that of a sorrowful and spindly mare?
Its neck being slung about like a loose, loose rope
by the force of the Bleak Bosom the horseman carries
 beneath his cloak.

Poor bumbling horse trotting through the monotony stink,
pulling not only the youthless grey mug the horseman has
 become
but also the strange and awful drag, drag,
that the horseman's torn and thrashed love life so sorrily
 lacks.

## FIVE THOUGHTS ON A NEW STREET

1.

In these houses, surrounded
with children yelling
'Water! Water! The curbs are dying!'
many a parental decadence dwells.

2.

The bricklayers know not what to do
but to sling their cement through the air
and Frisbee a wealth of new homes.

3.

What warm, good-doing
mothers let their children
play in this estate where
poets stroll in the midday
sun picking up toy-like
visions and storing them in poor
pockets but warm good-doing
mothers? What pavements,
but warm, good-doing pavements?
What fences but fences?

4.

In this
street there's
no 'Hare Krishna'
pouring from
the windows -

I do
miss it,
the incense filling
the air of
my last street.

**5.**

The smell of pork streams through these streets -
this, a suburban daydream with all of its own teeth.

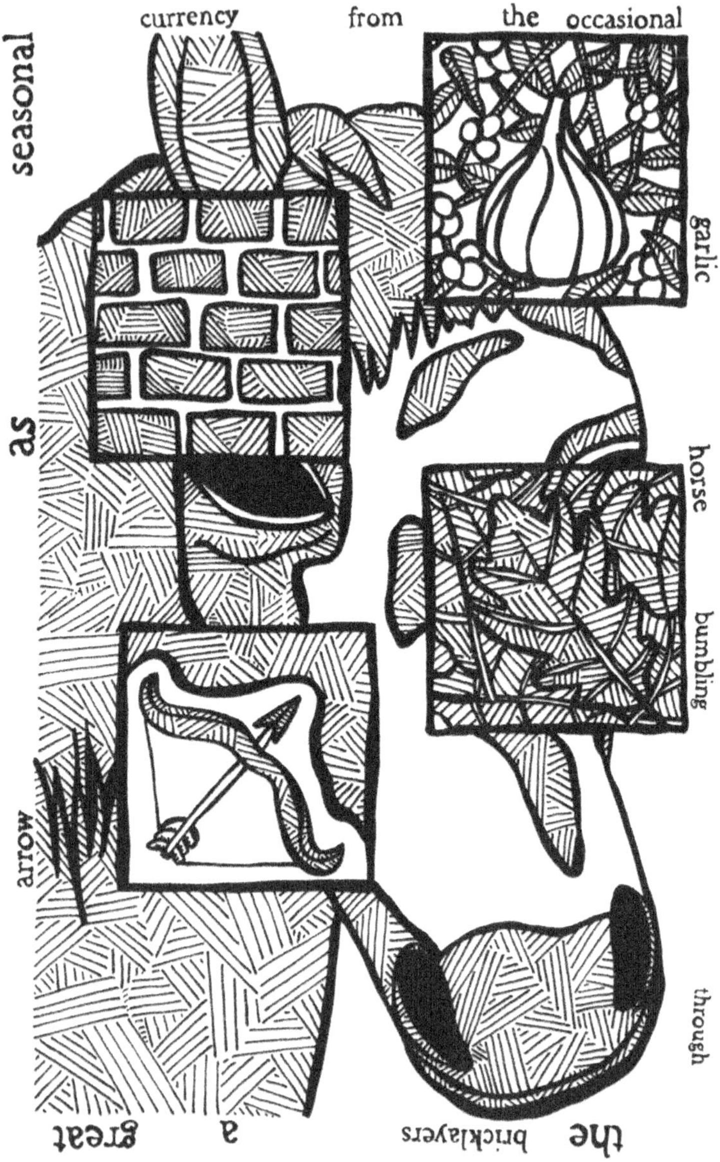
currency from the occasional
garlic horse bumbling through
the bricklayers a great
arrow as seasonal

## DIFFERENCE

In a star a man was born
like no other man
you have known before;
he had coarse teeth
and iced blood,
and when he bled
he bled a cherry Popsicle.
Said man slept in his star
like a good child
hidden under his bedding
with a pocket torch and a comic,
not sleeping.
Night after night
he contemplated life
and it's many hypocrisies
and constantly failed
to understand
why the moon was not on fire.

In the moon a woman was born
like no other woman
you have known before;
she had smooth gums
and lava blood,
and when she bled
she bled an exotic island.
Said woman slept in her moon
like a child,
tucked up so tightly,
sleeping with a nightlight on,
sound-O.
Night after night
she contemplated spirit
and its many good outcomes
and always succeeded
to understand

why the star was not dairy produce.

In non-existence a nothing was born
like no other nothing
you have known and loved,
it had false teeth, plastic gums
and lukewarm water blood,
and when it bled
it bled a spiced tea.
Said nothing slept in its non-existence
like an adult
with a high sex drive
and no one.
Night after night
it contemplated health
and its many obscenities,
and a good deal of the time
remained undecided
in accepting
the intentions of space and energy.

## HIS ALARM

Head heavy, buried deep
under a grey quilt
(a dull colour on a dull fabric),
he reached out far
from his woven winter mound
to grab for extra warmth,
the texture his shivery hand
landed upon undetermined
(cushioned, soft:
gerbilaic, toothed, a pet).
His legs thinning and weightless,
he floated, gutless,
on a long stream of air,
and the pet pulled him along
into the cloudless night
(to get a clearer look at himself).
There he saw them first,
people popping like pus
from each goose bump of his skin,
each asking for honey and crackers,
a happily-ever-after
(and the air-conditioning on)
to deepen them into sleep.
Stopping at a nearby chimney,
he obliged,
wiped them from his arms,
and saw them off as the pet flew them
into the wild night
(people pouring from their skins).
It went on, and on,
until all over the town,
layers of constant chatter
of people asking people
(asking people asking people)
for stories and snacks
eternally droned the streets.

Awoken by alarm,
thinking it a flash of fever,
he turned on the radio,
but honey and crackers
at a rapid frequency,
flying over the airwaves
(honey and crackers on all town quilts),
became a permanently frequent thing.
No 6am Schubert,
no 7am Tchaikovsky,
just a symphony of people
(and people and more people).
So, it was back to safe-and-sound for him,
begging a bed's forgiveness,
swearing on a saucer of Ovaltine,
and with only eyes
for the cold side of the pillow,
forgetting to set his alarm.

## MIDNIGHT

Sat up
cold, drinking milk,
listening to the tick
of midnight,
eyes watered,
chest thumped,
or rather, heart thumped,
got agitated,
looked to the ceiling,
saw nothing,
probably
a good job too,
couldn't imagine
seeing my own
reflection,
as if the ceiling
were a mirror,
no, keep that
for the mirror,
no need
to confuse things,
although
there was a fly
that shat itself
in black dots
like bad polka
all over the white
of the ceiling,
the ceiling
will never be the same again,
went to the computer,
edited another poem
in the collection,
added another poem
to the collection
about ferment and flies

and such,
swallowed hard
on the skin
of the hot milk,
wiped my lips
like a child,
went back to bed
thinking about something,
dead to the tock
of midnight.

## TWENTY FOUR

I turned twenty four
and I spent the day
thinking I should write
a birthday poem
as a document,

but apart from the one
about the young king
who zooms through bronze skies
on his pterodactyl,
there was no poem to write.

## LIFE SUDDENLY

Feeling the vines
of the sun
that wrap you
whole,

feeling the bells
of the wind
that knock you
toll,

feeling the stools
of the ground
that lift you
roll,

feeling your life
suddenly
as one strange
hole,

feeling the birds
above you
now on your
thumb,

feeling the sky
around you
now in your
gum,

feeling the God
amongst you
now hold your
plum,

feeling your life
suddenly
as one strange
sum,

feeling the steps
that ascend
turn into
rout,

feeling the trees
that grow tall
turn into
trout,

feeling the dew
that dampens
turn into
drought,

feeling your life
suddenly
as one strange
bout,

feeling the walls
that cascade
grow legs to
kick,

feeling the doors
that billow
grow tongues to
lick,

feeling the gates
that waver
grow bones to
pick,

feeling your life
suddenly
as one strange
click,

feeling your life
suddenly
as one strange
hit,

feeling your life
suddenly
as one weird
fit,

feeling your life
suddenly
as one odd
skit,

feeling your life,
suddenly
feeling your
life.

pterodactyl with false

teeth like a

torch fly the bed's plum

never zooms through on the

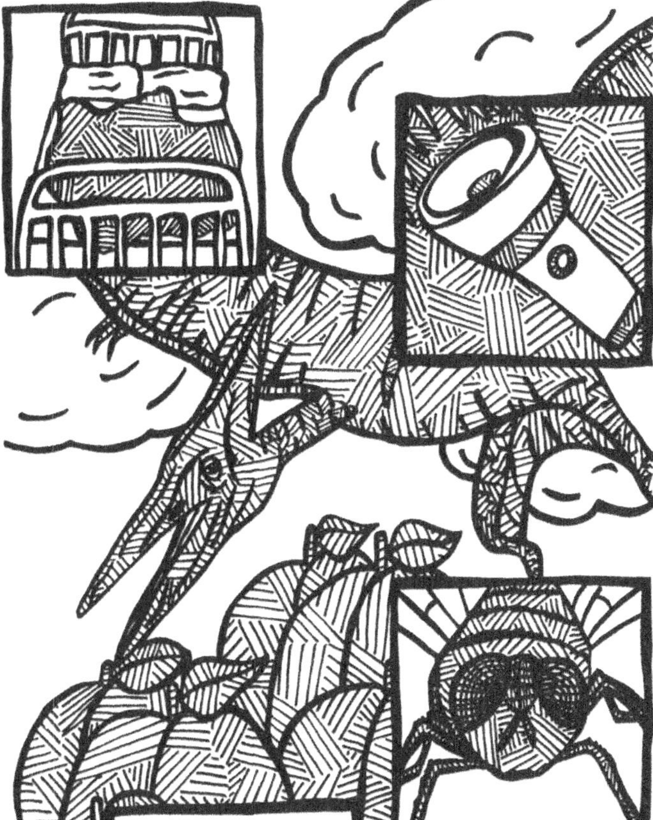

# THE DO-ANYTHINGNESS OF YOUTH

*A pre-mature retrospective of the Strangest Thankyou era of life, written over the course of this A.D. 2022.*

'Rook, What Secrets?' video shoot, 2010.
Photography by Daniel Gaine, Rook mask by Seany Tea,
Rook himself by R.C. Thomas.

## THE DO-ANYTHINGNESS OF YOUTH

1.

The poem is justified
whether aligned here or there
in body or brain.
A stanza wakes a soul,
its cadence pumps the heart.
Hyphens stitch up old wounds
where the line has come undone.
A semi-colon winks the poet
into an anesthetic slumber.
A poem can build the poet up
as much as it can break them down.
For a poem to level a poet out
it must be steam-roller heavy,
confident in its movement,
aware of its weight.
On a steep hill,
I unloaded Rook and tea poems
onto passing ears,
warranted or not.
I was told to move on
by a cantankerous shoe shop owner.
She boldly claimed
poems are of no talent,
but I made forty five pounds that morning,
with extra copper-plated steel,
when the Rook poured his fruity colours
from his chisel-cracked beak
(and between the loafers and the moccasins
I told her how many poems
it takes to write a good one,
how the simile
should be worshipped like a saint
[I'd hazard a guess
that she won't like this part

of this poem about her
not liking my poems, either.
Well, tough Birkenstocks.
Out into the world it runs]).
Bit by bit of me
flowed down the pavement,
gaining speed
and momentum with the morning,
unafraid, grabbing at language,
finding my own pace,
and I rolled through a puddle
of my own word-vomit.[1]
Now I load my poems back up,
I hold them secretly in my pockets,
no forty five pounds in them today,
just peaking poems out for air
every so often,
afraid to show my heart,
my white lilac,
the lungs I use to breathe
a careful comma
into a breathless space,

---

[1] Which reminds me: trolley alarm, composure commute, clicking four, glow verse, radiator tracks, roundabout choice, trouser paint, holiday vending, paper beak, organ cart, falafel summer, mud boat, crab stitches, mosaic crust, jazz stomp, armchair swing, Wednesday rice, happy apples, blueberry swim, brass owl, radio tapestry, squirrel union, calico walk, button charm, cold floor, pillowed day, false hands, always clock, password lunch, fish grunge, bike frame flank, sandalwood gods, townhouse swoop, narrow wax, bibliosmia pie, Valhalla knee, archive preach, island ease, pocket watch stars, stairway host, stretched castle, hill slide, slit sky, pancake solo, bygone embouchure, yore reed, big seeing, kettle beasts, water drag, chronic video, log start, flower peak, rental cake, palm chance, skull ploy, horse ceramic, monk barrage, paragon table, mess take, faded leaf.

until the hill presents itself
devoid of any junction.
A hard-faced cliff before me,
my options are to either jump
and hope my words
break my fall,
or let the wolves
of impending middle age
grab me by the ankles
with their petty teeth,
and drag me back through the muck
of tireless self-critique.

**2.**

In green surroundings,
I templated my own form,
pushing an unending pencil
through quiet woodland,
an ink-heavy pen
through a buttercup,
my stream-of-consciousness
through a river,
dripping with in-the-moment,
reflective verses
looking in on themselves
like open mirrors,
and out on the world
like curious periscopes,
and I sat bucolic,
a solitary white lilac,
writing away the nettles
and the tails of thorns
pinned to complicated donkeys,
desperate to unlock
the Rook's mind for myself
and sip the natural sugar
from its once sour, scraggy presence,

eyeing through the weeds
my dewy adulthood
greener still.[2]

3.

A notebook stroked in bracken,
a notebook thick with fern,
a notebook bathed in patio,
a notebook grazed in bark,
a notebook painted in sunshine,
a notebook gauzed in mist,
a notebook chalked with salt water,
a notebook wet with winter,
a notebook levelled with grasshopper,
a notebook hung with air,
a notebook trickled in stream,
a notebook glazed in oak,
a notebook taut with lawn,
a notebook glassed in greenhouse,
a notebook purposed in picnic,
a notebook soaked in daffodil,
a notebook masked in spring,
a notebook rooted in Rook,
a notebook grounded in granite,
a notebook skimmed in nightfall,
a notebook rolled in gatepost,
a notebook smoked with bridge,
a notebook spread in footpath,
a notebook vast with field,
a notebook piped in starlight,
a notebook broiled in summer,

---

[2] Which reminds me: a staircase steeped with watchful, cast iron goblins. My ankles heaved, toes bent. The night sitting at the top. Bright stars whitening, singing down 'Hallelujah, here it comes,' and then blinking its solar systems shut.

a notebook bright with beetle,
a notebook printed in moss,
a notebook joined with ginger,
a notebook dropped in fence,
a notebook loose with cloud,
a notebook shaded in apple,
a notebook doused in dust,
a notebook basked in dog,
a notebook armoured in autumn,
a notebook washed with white lilac,
pen in pocket, pen in place,
and a satchel of paper and pens.[3]

**4.**

I've written in the grass,
the river lowering
with the rise of the sun
on a pulley system.
I've written in internet cafes
with garlic mushrooms
underlining the Wi-Fi code.
I've written on a bench
eating hummus and oatcakes.
I've written knelt up to my bed
like a chairless, deskless freak.
I've written on a plane
with a dream of my late grandfather
riding along on the wing.
I've written whilst walking,
tripping over full stops.
I've written at the plots

---

[3] Which reminds me: the coil that keeps the pages together can't keep up. Where to put all this youthful paper? A loosening in the binding of a moleskin, too, lets the white lilacs in to smell the dried ink.

of dead poets.
I've written in gardens
with the sun swelling up around me.
I've written for the alchemy
of the Rook who looks on,
unphased,
alchemy commonplace,
holding on to secrets.
I've written on train station platforms
in the black of the night
(thinking I'd missed
my train by a day
or that I was sleeping),
with the coming and going
of quiet, shuffling strangers
with no need to write themselves
(those whose use a larynx
to communicate).
I've written on the train itself,
back and forth
between cow and man,
white lilac and tarmac,
grease and potpourri.
Now I write,
surrounded by houses,
looking out at a bird-feeder
bereft of little birds
to feast on its insides,
desperate to be dinner
just once.[4]

---

[4] Which reminds me: through the labyrinth of a crocheted star, down an aisle decked recklessly in cotton, and into a syrup cocoon, over and on and around again, people not stopping to ask their questions I have the answers to.

### 5.

'The poem must connect to the poem,
the mind be made up of the mind,
and all fuses must meet
to set the work alight.'
'Who says so?'
'The Rook does.'
I took things too seriously,
but that's just what your twenties will do,
criticism becomes more scathing
than it needs to be.
Just now
am I getting back to basics.
I'm throwing
three sheets to the wind.
In fact, I'm launching
a whole duvet set
with Egyptian quality cotton
into orbit
because I know Isis
will catch my every idea
and cradle it safe.
I'm saying 'fuck it,'
as many times as I like,
and the Rook caws 'fuck it,'
right back,
the notes echoing from the tip
of his winter mountain.
I'm including a feathered strawberry,
I'm letting the Roman pigeons eat,
and it's all fused together
because my mind makes it so.
And so it is so:
Cupid's arrow
blows through my hands,
and my early train,
up and down the railway line,

transports it home.
It's all connected,
as long as my same brain
is connected to my same body,
and as far as I'm aware
they're still attached.[5]

6.

For a time, *English Hair*,
freshly imported,
thick with keratin
and evening piazzas,
sourced from a muggy,
Italian summer cityscape
was the working title
of this little book I obsessed over,
and I was cocksure
about making it finite
(pulling and handing a strand,
and saying 'English Hair
[my nervous eyes
on my newly-Roman-dusted shoes].
There, there, there,
that's the title I'll use,
there's so much there in an English Hair...').[6]

---

[5] Which reminds me: from zipper to button, from Velcro to Sellotape, from glue to shoelace, from needle to thread, from staple to paperclip, from tag to binder clip, from hairclip to head band, from hair tie to plait, from plaid to tarmac, from cement to concrete, from clay to brick, from string to rope, from hillside to road, from stream to river, from boat to constellation, from contrails to potholes in the blue, to smoking leaves piling one on top of the other, white plumes feeding the deep, open mouth of the universe, its hollow belly growing bulbous and shooting everything out all at once in infinite directions.

It worked, but felt too regal,
the Rook of the mind denied it
(with myself as jury
and the Rook as judge
[how heavy-hammered
the poet's own mind is/
was the cynicism of age
already kicking in
at twenty four,
and ready to pop
at twenty five?]).
I thanked a strangeness
for naming the book
after itself instead.

**7.**

My body doesn't function
like it used to.
If you watch carefully,
you'll notice I wake up
much less to poem a dream
about the Rook
clawing the concrete
like a scheming beggar,
than to desperately try
to get the circulation in my legs
circulating again,
to peel off the sheets
from an overheated shell,
to keep track
of another aching bladder

---

[6] Which reminds me: from the dermal region of the second star to the right, follicles sprout idea trees, fruiting a matrix of flamingo-mermaid-horses and B movies called Minestrone Moon over and over again.

(and those are countless),
or to curse a bad back
which cries out for the Rook
to stamp his feet
all over it
and relieve the squalling ache.
And when will he come
with the fire hose,
his sirens wailing through the night,
to put out the burning
beneath my skin?
Days are cyclical,
ticking away slowly,
generally ending
where they started off,
and the closing credits
fall down the screen
of my living room window
in everyday-the-same order
of names and titles.
In the director's cut
there are failed takes of new scenes:
a breath doesn't blow me
as far as the top of a hill,
as much as I've heard
the view is good from up there.
A step doesn't walk me
to the end of a long road,
but I've heard the people
are nice in that part of the world.
My living room window
is a silent rendition
of a movie I was only ever

an extra in anyway.[7]
Extras are time,
and time is money
on this movie set called *Life*.

## 8.

I'm at the halfway mark
of my thirties
and I haven't seen much of them.
I've heard rumours of my thirties
floating about the place:
'I saw them counting
the loose hairs in their hands
mixed up with the conditioner
when they were taking a shower,'
'I heard they melted
when they saw the sun shine,'
'I heard they became glued icicles
when winter peeped
through the keyhole,'
'I heard they kept their receipt
and exchanged themselves
for a lesser-fitting size,'
'I saw them wandering,
wondering how to get back,'
'I saw them sat
in another waiting room

---

[7] Which reminds me: close-up. Endless actors pull faces at the camera lens which we all know is narrow enough to squash a worm to its actual size. Here comes said worm wriggling in the background, dispersing the soil wherever it needs to at the clapperboard's percussive demands. First it wriggles into the right hole, then it flees from the wrong hole. Zoom in to the worm. Zoom out. Pan right. Zoom in. More actors. They refuse to bow. Zoom out. Zoom out. Pan right. Zoom in. ZOOM IN. The popcorn morphs into a loud clock.

for the second time today,'
'I heard someone heard them
talking to someone,
who'd spoken to someone,
who knew someone else,
who'd heard someone mention
that they may or may have not
gone somewhere to see somebody
about something or other,
or something other,
but I don't know where.'
Who can you trust
as a reliable source
when time has vanished,
dispersed its two slender hands
into the void,
out of reach,
and anyone you ask
claims to say they had no part in it?
I put out a MISSING PERSON ad
but I've yet to receive
a substantial lead.[8]
I checked the kitchen cupboard
in case I misplaced them there.
No, just a lot of comfort food
that I cannot eat

---

[8] Which reminds me: five-foot-six. Wonky tooth. English Hair. Can turn neck to the right just slightly further than he can to the left. A nice selection of scars on the rear of his scalp. Both eyes relatively intact but can't read train times from a small distance un-eye-aided. Forever between facial hair arrangements. Enough physical complaints to share around. Interests include involuntary and uncomfortable silence. Often spotted fiddling with his face and any hair that may spring from it. Did speak once but choked on his words and fears the ordeal repeating itself. Call 0800-FOUND IN THE SAME PLACE WE LOST HIM immediately on retrieval of his body, mind, and soul as collected works.

in case my thirty-five-year-old stomach
falls out of its socket.
I enquired with the nurse
as to their whereabouts,
but she denied any involvement:
'I wasn't aware
they were even a thing for you
in the first place, Mr Thomas,
let alone so important
that misplacing them
would be an issue.'
I enquired with the Rook,
but no joy there either:
'Last time I saw your thirties,
they were looking pale
and heading for bed.'
I checked my bed,
nothing there.
I removed the sheets,
just the coldness of ghosts,
and the Rook had moved on
all humdrum and hungry,
a trail of white lilacs
memorialising his path.

9.

Two eyes now look up at me:
two poems.
Her small hand holds mine:
another poem.
Soft hair to stroke
and that really is soothing:
a whole book of poems
embodied in her nine-year-old self.
She comes to me,
unfolding her chatty blanket,
and from within it roll out

one hundred questions
on time and space,
closely followed
by her one hundred answers.
She knows evolution™,
she is evolution un-trademarked.[9]
She knows Mars,
knows parallel universes,
knows multiverses,
knows the singular universe, too.
She probes for more information
about the possibility
of growing a second human brain,
and doesn't sit back
but drinks up the knowledge,
glugging it thirstily
from a Darwinian goblet
that jumps out from the sea
with a 'Cheers to you,'
and scampers off
to discover fire
(knowledge of which
I give her what I have
[and she knowing Google]).
She asks about linguistics
and which way
the human tongue may twist
as the years go by,
or whether we'll have a tongue,

---

[9] Which reminds me: grow bags in the sun fill themselves with yellow diamonds. They borrow sunrays for legs which they stick into the compost. They sway back and forth in the cool air and a breeze, already passing, pinches a tiny hold of them, squeezes and stretches them through a gentle mangle. Watch them elongate. A tiny Martian stops by and decks them out in all the things they need. Necks, eyes, a handy spinal cord, hands, a choice of watch. They walk now on two feet.

have a language at all.
Saturday park people
walk by with curious eyebrows,
kind smiles,
or their mouths making circles,
you've-got-yourself-a-thinker-there
faces on them
(and I wonder whether
we'll take the language
of the Rook for our own
[with Isis nursing our larynxes
that bloom white lilacs]).
I know the universe did me well,
singular, multiverse,
parallel, or daughter universe,
gracing me with an Emmeline,
a poem too pure to write.

**10.**

The Rook lowers his beak
from a wooden cart,
cocks his head
at the concrete,
enters a train station
platform photo booth,
vanishes in a flash,
leaving his cosmic feathers
in a platform photo booth
where the last photo taken
shows him with human fingers,
his blackened fingernails
tapping madly at the screen
for another chance
to try to not blink again.
On the other side
of the platform photo booth
he rolls eggs

from a cheap carton,
twines his broomstick wings
around commuters,
twists his twiggy legs,
walks crookedly,
retreats to his nest,
and scraps his poem.[10]
I was a Rook once.
With my old poems
handed to a train station
ticket inspector,
I hopped on board and left,
egged out
a *Strangest Thankyou* instead.
One day, I'll return,
re-live that old,
unfavoured Rook poem,
apologise
for not sprucing him up
the way I could have done,
put a white bow on his wise head,
look him earnestly
in those glazed stone eyes,
deep and metamorphic,
and make the plea
for a resurgence
in the do-anythingness of youth.

---

[10] Which reminds me: lonely, a punctuation mark falls out of its nest, a noun grabs at twigs on its way down, an adjective calls out to a nearby tawny owl for help but goes unheard, verbs play a game of noughts and crosses with the moon as they see it fall between branches. Cuts, grazes, undone laces. The alphabet's plural unloads itself with a ready stretcher from the back of an ambulance.

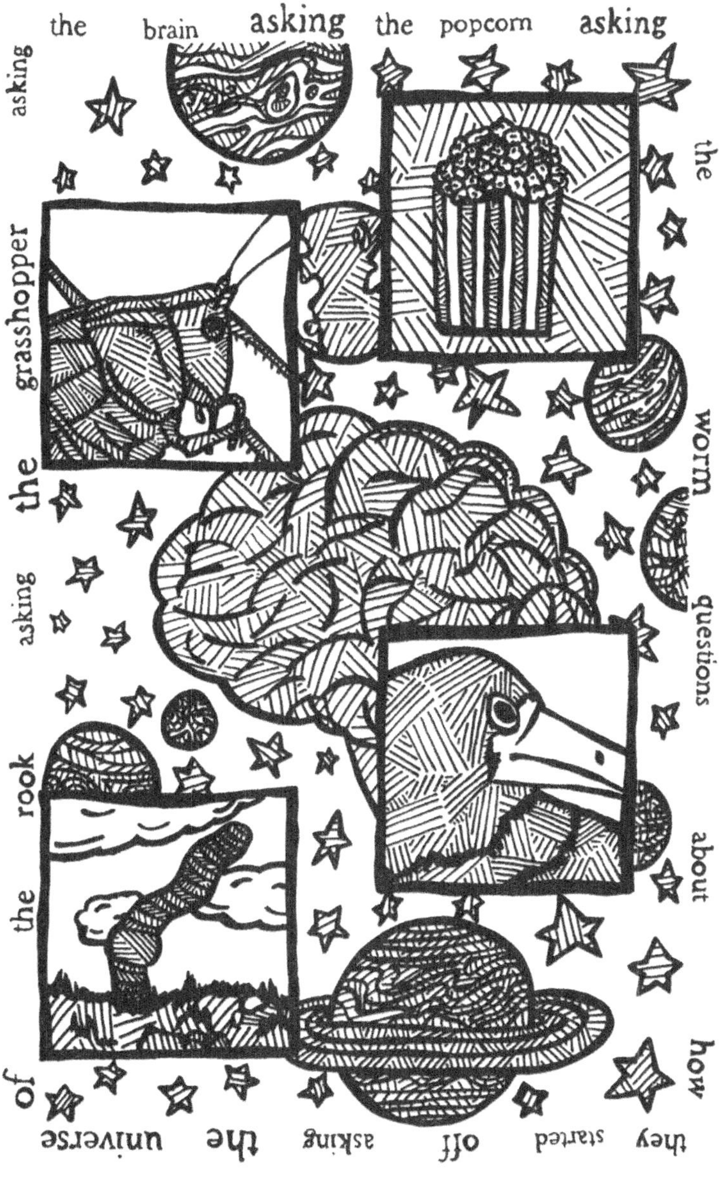
asking the brain asking the popcorn asking
the worm questions about how
they started off asking the universe
of the rook asking the grasshopper asking

## ACKNOWLEDGEMENTS

Thanks to Maria C. McCarthy and Bob Carling who ran Cultured Llama for welcoming me into their stable and publishing the first incarnation of this book in 2012, and for their continued support. Thanks to everyone who bought, read, endorsed, or supported this book's original incarnation in any way. Thanks to all those who have continued to support me in this undertaking of its reincarnation.

Some of these poems previously appeared in the following print and online journals and anthologies under the name Richard Thomas: Bottlerockets, The Coffeehouse, Fire, Homeless Diamonds, The IMPpress, Neon Highway, The Oddrot, Orbis, Reflections, Scarlet Dragonfly Journal, Symmetry Pebbles, Unexplored Territory (ed. Maria C. McCarthy), Venus in Scorpio, and Weyfarers.


## HEY READER

You made it to the end of the book! For that, I'm entirely grateful! Now you've come this far, could I ask for just one more thing? Would you consider leaving a review on Amazon, Goodreads, or wherever else you like to review books? Or perhaps you could take a screenshot and send it to me, and/or tag me in a social media post or story. All of this really helps a poet out (we're a struggling breed). In return, I'll send you a discount code to use in my shop:
rcthomasthings.com


**Email:** hi@rcthomasthings.com
**Socials:** rcthomasthings

Printed in Great Britain
by Amazon

24887956R00078